Greedy Stanley

Sandra Andrews

"Today is my birthday," shouted Terry.
"And I am going to choose a pet of my own!"

At the petshop there were rabbits.
"Too furry," thought Terry.

There was a tortoise munching a cabbage leaf.
"Too boring," thought Terry.

A parrot was sitting on a perch.
"Too noisy," shouted Terry.

There was a fish in a bowl.
"You can't play with a fish," sighed Terry.

Then Terry saw a basket in a corner.
Inside was a brightly coloured snake.

"His name is Stanley," said the shopkeeper.
"But wouldn't you rather have a puppy?"
"No," said Terry.
"I'd like to have Stanley, please."

When they arrived home, Terry's Mum thought that Stanley might be hungry.

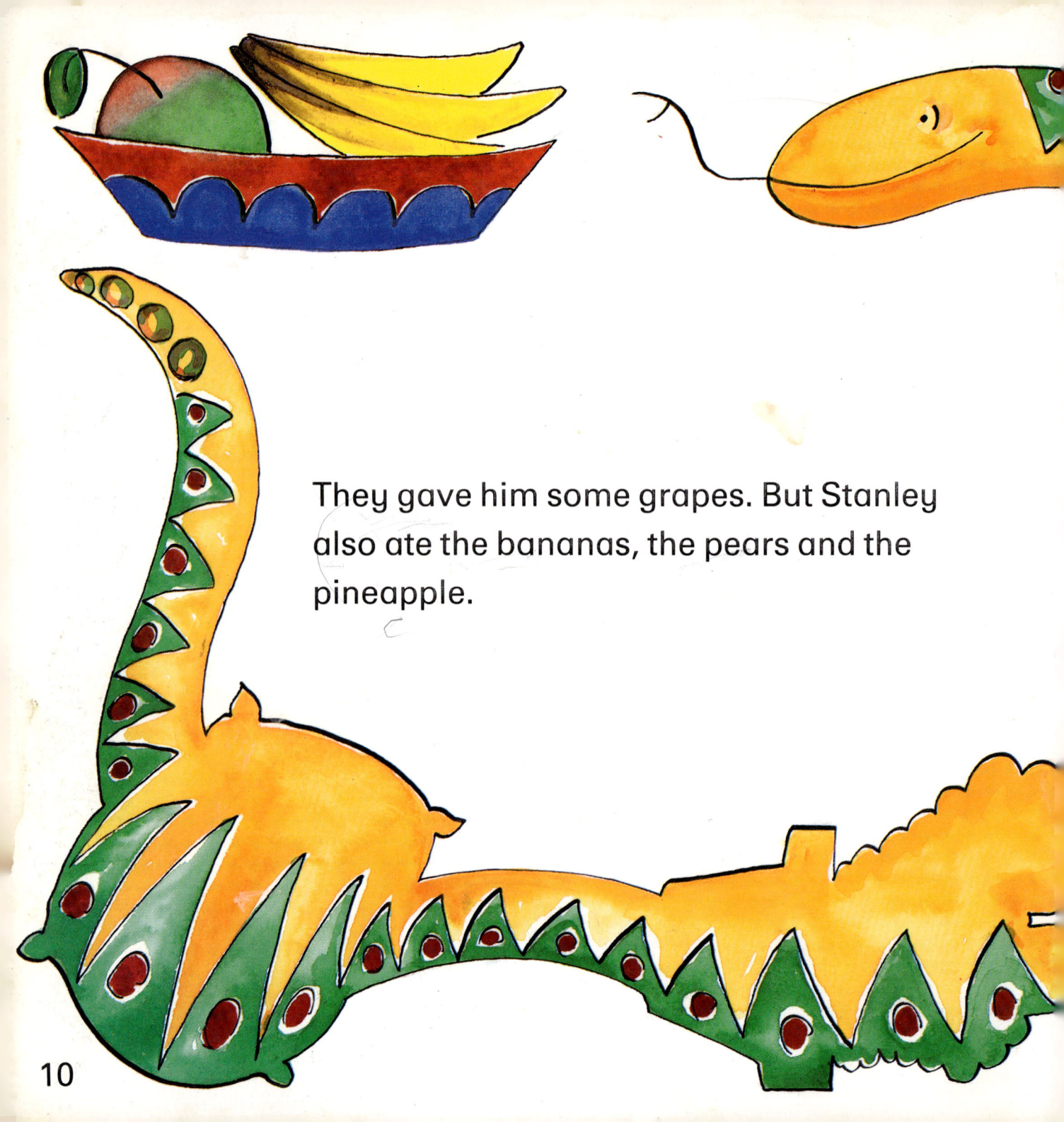

They gave him some grapes. But Stanley also ate the bananas, the pears and the pineapple.

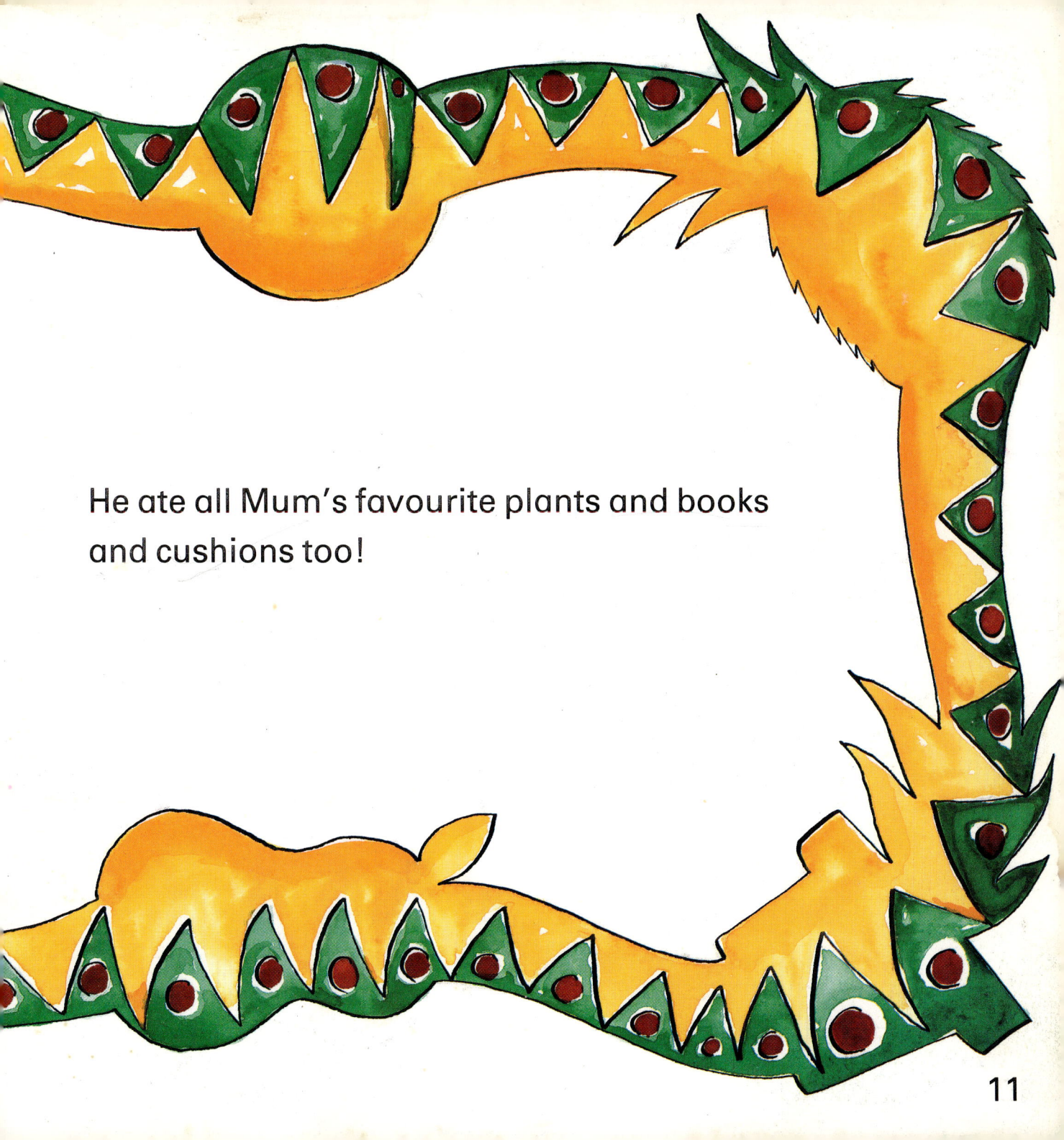

He ate all Mum's favourite plants and books and cushions too!

They tried to catch greedy Stanley.
But he kept wriggling away.
What could they do?

13

Stanley rushed into his basket and gulped down the cake.

Before he could escape, they put the lid on the basket.

"I think for my next birthday I will have a rabbit after all," said Terry.